"Rusty Meek's *Ecc[lesiastes and the Up]side-Down World* invites us all to engage with this book from antiquity that speaks to the struggle of meaning-making in the complicated condition we find ourselves in today. His writing is intensely personal and creatively accessible, drawing us as readers into a deep encounter with the wisdom found in this book. Don't pass up this opportunity to engage with this timely book."

—Mark J. Boda, Professor of Old Testament
McMaster Divinity College, Ontario, Canada

"We live in a fallen world and struggle with finding meaning in life. Russell Meek insightfully explores the book of Ecclesiastes, sharing his own difficulties while explaining why this fascinating biblical book speaks to us all in the midst of our problems. Well written, accessible, and theologically profound, I enthusiastically recommend this book for all people who want to grow in their faith and resilience in a difficult world."

—Tremper Longman III, Distinguished Scholar
Professor Emeritus of Biblical Studies, Westmont College

"Ecclesiastes is confusing, often frustrating, and sometimes demoralizing. So is life. And yet, with disarming honesty and engaging authenticity, Meek weaves his life struggles into his interpretation of Ecclesiastes to create a tapestry of hope. Holding the text under the microscope of careful exegesis, he enables readers to see how threads from the rest of the Hebrew Bible, particularly Genesis, give the book's gloomy lines a brighter hue."

—Will Kynes, Associate Professor of Biblical Studies
Department of Biblical and Religious Studies
Samford University

"Ecclesiastes has always been my favorite book of the Bible. Now I love it—and understand it—even more because of Russ Meek's knowledgeable and lovely exposition. Meek draws connections to the greater plan unfolded in the whole of scripture showing, once again, how every word of God's word matters."

—Karen Swallow Prior, Research Professor of English and Christianity & Culture Southeastern Baptist Theological Seminary author of *On Reading Well: Finding the Good Life through Great Books*

"Some commentaries are pastoral, others are exegetical. Russ Meek manages to be both, as well as personal, in this little book on Ecclesiastes. You'll be heartened by hearing his story and strengthened in your faith as you come to terms with the message of Ecclesiastes, as told by this accomplished author and scholar."

—Jason K. Allen, President Midwestern Baptist Theological Seminary and Spurgeon College

ECCLESIASTES
AND THE SEARCH FOR MEANING IN AN UPSIDE-DOWN
WORLD

RUSSELL L. MEEK

HENDRICKSON
PUBLISHERS

an imprint of Hendrickson Publishing Group

Ecclesiastes and the Search for Meaning in an Upside-Down World

© 2022 Russell L. Meek

Published by Hendrickson Publishers
an imprint of Hendrickson Publishing Group
Hendrickson Publishers, LLC
P. O. Box 3473
Peabody, Massachusetts 01961–3473
www.hendricksonpublishinggroup.com

ISBN 978-1-68307-416-8

All rights reserved. No part of this book may be reproduced or transmitted in any form or by any means, electronic or mechanical, including photocopying, recording, or by any information storage and retrieval system, without permission in writing from the publisher.

Unless otherwise designated, Scripture quotations contained herein are taken from the author's own translation.

Scripture quotations marked CSB®, are taken from the Christian Standard Bible®, Copyright © 1999, 2000, 2002, 2003, 2009, 2017 by Holman Bible Publishers. Used by permission. CSB® is a federally registered trademark of Holman Bible Publishers.

Scripture quotations marked (ESV) are taken from the Holy Bible, English Standard Version (ESV®), copyright © 2001 by Crossway, a publishing ministry of Good News Publishers. Used by permission. All rights reserved.

Scripture quotations marked (NASB) are taken from the New American Standard Bible®, Copyright © 1960, 1962, 1963, 1968, 1971, 1972, 1973, 1975, 1977, 1995 by The Lockman Foundation. Used by permission. (www.lockman.org)

Quotations designated (NET) are from the NET Bible® copyright ©1996–2016 by Biblical Studies Press, L.L.C. All rights reserved.

Scripture quotations marked (NIV) are taken from the Holy Bible, New International Version®, NIV®. Copyright © 1973, 1978, 1984, 2011 by Biblica, Inc.™ Used by permission of Zondervan. All rights reserved worldwide. www.zondervan.com. The "NIV" and "New International Version" are trademarks registered in the United States Patent and Trademark Office by Biblica, Inc.™

Scripture quotations marked NKJV are taken from the New King James Version®. Copyright © 1982 by Thomas Nelson. Used by permission. All rights reserved.

Scripture quotations marked (NLT) are taken from the Holy Bible, New Living Translation, copyright ©1996, 2004, 2015 by Tyndale House Foundation. Used by permission of Tyndale House Publishers, Inc., Carol Stream, Illinois 60188. All rights reserved.

Cover photo by Louis Maniquet on unsplash

Printed in the United States of America

First Printing — February 2022

For my wife and sons: My goodness, I love y'all.

Ari, may God make you strong and brave like a lion.

*Abel, may God give you the courage and faithfulness
to always bring your best to God,
no matter what.*

*Elijah, may God give you the boldness and fortitude
to speak truth to power.*

*And Brittany, you convince me more every day that
"he who finds a wife finds a good thing,
and has obtained favor from Yahweh" (Prov 18:22).*

CONTENTS

Preface — ix

1. **The Genesis Shape of Ecclesiastes** — 1

   Qohelet, the author of Ecclesiastes, is no skeptic or cynic. Rather, he a wise man trying to navigate a life that often doesn't make sense. To fully understand what this wise man is telling us, we have to see how he uses Genesis to frame his discussion of life, death, God, and humanity.

2. **Abel and the Meaning of *Hebel*** — 29

   Often translated "vanity" or "meaningless," the key word *hebel* is actually the name "Abel" in Hebrew. Qohelet uses *hebel* as a metaphor to cause us to reflect on how the injustice and transience of Abel's life marks everything "under the sun."

3. **From Here, Where? Fear God and Enjoy His Gifts**   51

> Qohelet doesn't shy away from the realities of living in a post-fall, sin-ridden, upside-down world marked by Abel-like experiences. Qohelet goes beyond acknowledging this reality to light a path through life for us. In short, we navigate the Abel-ness of life by living in relationship with God and enjoying the gifts he gives us.

PREFACE

Hi, I'm Russ. I'm a husband, a dad of three sons, and an Old Testament professor. This book is a small part of a bigger story of how God used the Old Testament to save my faith, and to save my life. I grew up in church, and I became a Christian when I was eighteen or so—shortly before my freshman year of college. I started using drugs when I was around twelve years old, just after my grandmother died, and that way of facing life stayed with me for a long, long time. I know a lot of people who became Christians and left behind a life of addiction, but it didn't happen that way for me. I had periods of sobriety, some lasting longer than others, but drugs remained my primary method for alleviating the pain and anxiety that you'll read about in this book. I've been drug-free for more than twelve years as of this writing, but I have no illusions about the darkness that lurks within me and still cries out to be fed from time to time.

This book isn't about addiction, but I think it's important for you to know this part of my story because that way of coping with the upside-downness of life ran for a while in parallel with my study of Ecclesiastes. All through my master's degree, when I first started to study Ecclesiastes with a former mentor, I was high as a kite. Though God was starting to show me that Scripture offers a way of understanding suffering and seeing our way through it, I still clutched opiates to numb my heart and mind. So even though I don't talk about that part of my life in this book, it lingers there in the background.

I started to study Ecclesiastes because I thought I found in it a kindred spirit who, like me, had thrown up his hands and given up on faith and life, who had accepted the meaninglessness of these years on planet Earth and was simply waiting out the time until death would free him. What I found instead—with the help of that former mentor I mentioned—was a path through life that doesn't involve the bottom of a pill bottle. So, that's what this book is about: How Ecclesiastes taught me to navigate life, with all of its confusion and frustration and suffering, in a way that pleases God. I hope I can convince you to read Ecclesiastes in the same way.

Russell L. Meek
Sandpoint, Idaho
2021

Chapter 1

THE GENESIS SHAPE OF ECCLESIASTES

My folks split when I was six years old. Dad, a serial adulterer, finally left my mom to make an honest woman of his mistress. My older brother took me on a drive just before my dad moved out of our house, and our paths crossed on the two-lane road that led out of town.

"Where's Dad going?" I asked my brother.

"He'll be back."

He wouldn't.

That sort of pain is hard to verbalize. If you've experienced it, then you know how I felt. I'm grateful if you don't know. Half a decade later, my grandmother passed away. She'd stepped into the gaping hole my father left, which made her death all the more devastating. In those years of my life, I somehow missed a crucial lesson: It's important to express your emotions, to give voice to your heartache and rage, to let it all out in some way. A year or so after my grandmother died, though, I found several voices I could relate to.

"Blacks aren't like us," my dad once told me, with a seriousness that only a deep-South racist could muster. He went on to tell me that, while it was fine to work alongside Black Americans, there must be a clear separation in all other areas of life. "We're just different," he would say. "We're made different. We think different."

So you can imagine my dad's surprise upon learning that the only thing keeping his young son sane was some cassette tapes of N.W.A., Eazy-E, Bone Thugs-N-Harmony, and later Jay-Z, Eminem, and Dr. Dre. Now, my students laugh when I tell them gangsta rap saved my life. But it did. It gave me the language I needed at the time to express the anger boiling inside of me.

In the years since I first passed money to my older brother so he could buy me the tapes labeled Parental Advisory: Explicit Lyrics, I've learned quite a bit more about the value of hip hop. One of its significant features is that it relies heavily on allusion to connect with listeners and to communicate a whole world of cultural context needed to really get what the artist is saying.

Take the Jay-Z song "Moment of Clarity," for example. It's filled with clever wordplay, rhymes, and allusions to Jay-Z's previous work, other hip-hop artists, his own life story, the war on drugs, prison culture, and music industry awards. It's a masterpiece of songwriting and cultural commentary. When I play the song for students in my classes, they are familiar enough with popular culture that they have no problem pointing out the song's allusions and describing the backstory, which is necessary for fully understanding what Jay-Z is getting at in the song. Can I listen to and appreciate the song without knowing who Common or Biggie Smalls are, or what "platinum" refers to, or even what "four scores and seven years ago" evokes, or noticing that in one stanza he moves from squares to circles to triangles? Sure. But my understanding will be severely truncated, and I definitely won't appreciate the songwriting genius that went into those four minutes and twenty-four seconds.

Some years after I discovered rap, I was introduced to Ecclesiastes. That book, more than gangsta rap ever could, showed me how to navigate the grief and anguish life brings. And the author of that book, Qohelet (rendered "Teacher" or "Preacher" by some English translations), does the very same thing as Jay-Z, or rather Jay-Z does the same thing as Qohelet. Ecclesiastes (from the Greek equivalent of the Hebrew word Qohelet, both of which seem to mean "member of an assembly" or "assembly," respectively) is filled with allusions—specifically, to the book of Genesis—and if we don't pick up on those allusions, then we'll miss what Qohelet is trying to do with what he is saying. Just as my students are so steeped in popular culture that they can't help but notice the allusions in Jay-Z's "Moment of Clarity," Qohelet's original readers were so steeped in their own culture—a large part of which included the Torah (the Pentateuch), or first five books of the Old Testament—that they couldn't help but pick up on the connections he was making to Genesis. So, in order for us to be ideal readers, we must likewise spend time in the book of Genesis.

In this chapter, I'm going to talk about several of the allusions to Genesis in Ecclesiastes so that we can better understand the book and its application to our modern lives. But don't just take my word for it: open up your Bible and come along with me (especially since I'm using my own translation of the Hebrew text to highlight repeated terms that English translations often obscure). Keep an eye out for repeated vocabulary and themes. These are the breadcrumbs that Qohelet has dropped along the way to let us know where he's been.

TREES AND WATER AND PARKS, OH MY!

In Ecclesiastes 2, Qohelet is in the midst of describing the various things he tried in order to determine what "was good for humans to do under heaven during the few days of their life" (v. 3). These verses are nestled in what scholar James Crenshaw has called Qohelet's "Royal Experiment."[1] It's this passage (Eccl 2:1–12) that has made many readers throughout history think that Solomon wrote Ecclesiastes, even though the book itself contains no overt claim to authorship.[2] Qohelet has already experimented with

---

1. James L. Crenshaw, *Ecclesiastes*, Old Testament Library (Philadelphia: Westminster, 1987), 68.
2. See the discussion in Russell L. Meek, "'I Was King over Israel in Jerusalem': Inerrancy and Authorial Ambiguity in Eccle-

pleasure and laughter and folly and wine, and now he comes to a grand building project that evokes images of God's work in the garden of Eden:

> I made great works for myself. I built for myself houses, I planted for myself vineyards. I made for myself gardens and parks, and I planted in them trees of every kind. I made for myself ponds of water from which to water the forest of sprouting trees.
> (Eccl 2:4–6)

Now let's look at a few verses from the narrative where God creates the garden of Eden:

> And on the seventh day God finished his work that he had done. And he rested on the seventh day from all the work that he had done. ... And Yahweh God planted a garden from east in Eden, and he put there the man whom he had formed. And Yahweh God caused to sprout from the ground every tree desirable to sight and good for food. The tree of life was in the midst of the garden, as was the tree of the knowledge of good and evil.
>
> And a river went out from Eden to water the garden, and from there it divided and became four heads.
> (Gen 2:2, 8–10)

---

siastes," *Journal for the Evangelical Study of the Old Testament* 4 (2015): 63–85.

In the span of only a few verses, Qohelet uses eight terms taken from Genesis to describe the garden he made for himself.[3] Qohelet "plants" a vineyard and a "garden" with trees "of every kind" (see also Gen 1:11–12, 29; 2:9, 16–17). In both Genesis and Ecclesiastes, the planted trees "sprout," and Qohelet "watered" his gardens and vineyards with a system of pools just as God "watered" Eden (Gen 2:10). Finally, Qohelet "made" all of this, just as God "made" his garden in Genesis.[4]

	Ecclesiastes 2:4–6	**Genesis 2:2, 8–10**
Repeated terms	"to plant" (2x)	"to plant"
	"to make" (2x)	"to make" (2x)
	gardens	garden (3x)
	trees of every kind of fruit	trees of every kind
	"to water"	"to water"
	"to sprout"	"to sprout"
Repeated themes	creation of a garden by a ruler	creation of a garden by a ruler

TABLE 1.1. Allusion in Ecclesiastes 2:4–6 to Genesis 2:2, 8–10

---

3. Arian Verheij ("Paradise Retried: On Qohelet 2:4–6," *Journal for the Study of the Old Testament* 50 [1991]: 113–15) outlines the linguistic similarities and thematic parallels between this passage and the first chapters of Genesis.

4. The verb is also repeated in Gen 1:7, 16, 25–26, 31; 2:3–4, 18.

These repeated terms are common, to be sure, but the sheer volume of repeated vocabulary is significant. As Arian Verheij has pointed out, "Taken separately, these words are not remarkable: for the most part they are indeed very common in Biblical Hebrew. It is their combined occurrence here and in Genesis that establishes a firm link between the texts."[5]

Beyond the overlapping vocabulary, the themes in Genesis and Ecclesiastes run parallel to each other—both contexts recount the creation of a garden by a great ruler, though of course Qohelet's greatness and that of his garden pales in comparison with the work that God did in those six days at the beginning of time.

Some scholars argue that Qohelet in this passage is not relying on Genesis for his garden imagery but that he is simply employing a common ancient Near Eastern motif of garden building by great monarchs.[6] For example, one artifact (the Tell Siran bottle) tells us that the ancient ruler Amminadab built a garden and a vineyard,[7] which were common in upper-class

---

5. Verheij, "Paradise Retried," 114.

6. See P. T. Crocker, "'I Made Gardens and Parks . . . ,'" *Buried History* 26 (1990): 20–23.

7. Craig Bartholomew, *Ecclesiastes*, Baker Commentary on the Old Testament Wisdom and Psalms (Grand Rapids: Baker Academic, 2009), 132. See H. O. Thompson and F. Zayadine, "The Tell Siran Inscription," *BASOR* 212 (1973): 5–11; Fawzi Zayadine, "La Bouteille de Tell Sirân," *Le Monde de la Bible* 46 (1986): 22–23. See also "Instruction of Merikare" in *Ancient Egyptian Literature: A Book of Readings*, ed. Miriam Lichtheim, 3 vols (Berkeley: University of California Press), 1:97–109; "Instruction of King Amenhemnet," in the same, 1:135–9. For further examination of

residences of ancient Mesopotamia and Egypt.[8] Allusion to this broader theme is likely, particularly since these verses seem to allude to the story of Solomon's great wealth and power.[9]

But the fuller ancient Near Eastern context of garden building by rulers does not detract from the fact that Qohelet uses language lifted directly from the garden of Eden narrative, which is a much closer—and therefore more likely—source for the book of Ecclesiastes.

EVERYTHING APPROPRIATE IN ITS TIME

Ecclesiastes 3:1 provides our next reference to the book of Genesis. Here Qohelet states, "[God] made

---

the relationship between Qohelet's royal description and wider ancient Near Eastern royal literature and inscriptions, see Kurt Galling, "Koheleth-Studien," *Zeitschrift für die alttestamentliche Wissenschaft* 50 (1932): 276–99; Gehard von Rad, *Wisdom in Israel* (London: Bloomsbury, 1993), 226; Christoph Uehlinger, "Qohelet im Horizont mesopotamischer, levantinischer und ägyptischer Weisheitsliteratur der persischen und hellenistichen Zeit," in *Das Buch Kohelet*, ed. L. Schwienhorst-Schönberger (Berlin: de Gruyter, 1997), 155–247. See also Crenshaw, *Ecclesiastes*, 79. He points to Song 4:12; 5:1; 6:2, 11, and Neh 2:8 as other indications that park building was significant in the Old Testament. In addition, he sees the Siloam inscription and the Moabite Stone as further indicators of the larger ancient Near Eastern motif of garden building among the wealthy.

8. Bartholomew, *Ecclesiastes*, 132.

9. See C. L. Seow, *Ecclesiastes*, Anchor Bible 18C (New York: Doubleday, 1997), 150; however, note Weeks's objection in Stuart Weeks, *Ecclesiastes and Scepticism*, The Library of Hebrew Bible/Old Testamnet Studies 541 (London: T&T Clark, 2012), 24–27.

everything appropriate in its time. He has also set eternity in their heart so that humans cannot discover the work that God made from beginning until end." This verse seems to allude to a number of verses in Genesis 1, but verse 31 serves as a representative example: "And God saw all that he had made, and behold, it was very good."

There are three words shared in these two verses (not including the ubiquitous term "that"): "to make," "all," and "God." As in the previous passage in Ecclesiastes, we are dealing with very common terms in the Old Testament.

Nevertheless, the overlapping thematic elements between the two passages make it likely that Ecclesiastes is alluding to the creation account in Genesis. At the very least, both passages describe creation with similar vocabulary and come to similar conclusions.

This is enough to give us pause and prompt us to consider whether and why Ecclesiastes might be compelling us to think about God's initial creation event.

ASHES TO ASHES, DUST TO DUST

Qohelet is not shy when it comes to talking about death, and in two places he uses language straight from Genesis. In 3:16–21, Qohelet is lamenting the sad fate that awaits humans and animals alike when he states,

> All are going to the same place; all are from the dust and all return to the dust.
> (Eccl 3:20)

	Ecclesiastes 3:11	**Genesis 1**
Repeated terms	all	all
	"to make"	"to make"
	the God	God
Approximate synonyms	appropriate/beautiful	good
Repeated interconnected themes	creation	creation
	God as agent of creation	God as agent of creation
	creation viewed positively	creation viewed positively

Table 1.2. Allusions in Ecclesiastes 3:11 to Genesis 1

Later, at the conclusion of the well-known poem that closes out the book, Qohelet states,

> Then the dust will return upon the earth as it was, and the breath will return to God who gave it.
>
> (Eccl 12:7)

These two passages use language similar to what we find in the book of Genesis, first in reference to the creation of Adam and then in reference to the curse of death that resulted from the first sin.

> Then Yahweh Elohim formed the man of dust from the ground and breathed in his nostrils

the breath of life. And the man became a living being.

> (Gen 2:7)

By the sweat of your face you will eat bread until you return to the ground from which you were taken, for dust you are and to dust you will return.

> (Gen 3:19)

The charts above and below summarize the overlapping vocabulary and corresponding thematic elements. Given the subject matter and preponderance of shared vocabulary, the allusions in Ecclesiastes can hardly be coincidental.

It is significant that Qohelet draws heavily on the book of Genesis for his theology of death. Qohelet uses the "dust" language in 3:18–21 to support his most shocking argument: That in the end, death levels the field even between humans and animals. He returns to this imagery to conclude both his poem about death and dying and the body of the book (Eccl 12:7): "And the dust returns upon the earth as it was, and the breath will return to the God who gave it."

Qohelet's last statement sums up his view of human life—it begins in dust and ends in dust—and likely answers the question posed in 3:21: "Who knows if the breath of humans goes upward and the breath of animals goes downward to the earth?" God knows!

In sum, Qohelet uses language and themes from Genesis to support his intertwined theology and anthropology: God, the creator, formed humans from

	Ecclesiastes 3:18–21	Genesis 2:7	Genesis 3:19
Repeated terms	the man (4x)	the man (2x)	
	the God	God	
	the dust	dust	dust
	"to return"		"to return" (2x)
Approximate synonyms	breath/spirit (3x)	breath of life	
Syntactical features	"the man" is a passive recipient	"the man" is a passive recipient	"the man" is a passive recipient
	"the man" is "from dust"	"the man" is "from dust"	"the man" is "from dust"
	transposition of terms from Gen 3:19		
		the man will "return" "to dust"	the man will "return" "to dust"
	The repeated terms and approximate synonyms figure prominently in their respective contexts		
Repeated themes	creation of humans from dust	creation of humans from dust	creation of humans from dust
	return of humans to dust upon death		return of humans to dust upon death

TABLE 1.3. Allusion in Ecclesiastes 3:18–21

	Ecclesiastes 12:7	**Genesis 2:7**	**Genesis 3:19**
Repeated terms	the dust	dust	dust (2x)
	the God	God	
	"to return" (2x)		"to return" (2x)
Approximate synonyms	the earth	the ground	the ground
	breath/spirit	breath of life	
Syntactical features	*Repeated terms and approximate synonyms figure prominently*		
	dust is from the earth/ground	dust is from the earth/ground	dust is from the earth/ground
	God is giver of breath	God is giver of breath	
Repeated Themes	matter from which life was created	matter from which life was created	matter from which life was created
	creation of life	creation of life	creation of life
	dissolution of life		dissolution of life
	matter to which life will return		matter to which life will return

Table 1.4. Allusion in Ecclesiastes 12:7

the dust. And yet death remains inescapable, which, as we'll see later, makes it all the more imperative that we enjoy God's gifts.

There are several moving parts in 3:16–21, where Qohelet addresses the issues of injustice during this life, ultimate justice in the life to come, death (which seems to make everything moot anyway), and enjoyment in our present moment. Part of his use of Genesis in this passage is to explain both the original intent of work and the effects of sin on work. He subtly reminds us of the curses that came from Adam and Eve's sin. The most crushing of these is death, but it's also important to remember that the curse has hindered humanity's ability to take pleasure in work—one of the four gifts from God that Qohelet commends (see below). Although there is joy in work and God will ultimately judge the wicked, it remains impossible for any of us to escape the stench of death (e.g., Eccl 2:11, 18).

In 12:17, Qohelet alludes to creation and the curse to indicate that:

1. God is the sovereign creator of all things, and

2. the eventual fate of humanity is its own doing.

By using these particular texts from Genesis, Qohelet forces to our minds Genesis 1–2, which describes when God created everything "good," and Genesis 3, which describes when everything went wrong. Further, Qohelet is essentially answering his own question about death—why?—by turning us to Genesis: human sin is responsible for human death.

CARPE DIEM AND THE QUEST FOR EDEN

Seven passages in Ecclesiastes (2:24–26; 3:10–15, 16–22; 5:18–20; 8:10–15; 9:7–10; 11:8–10) call for us to take joy in various aspects of life—the same aspects of life we find the original humans enjoying in the garden (Gen 2:15–25). As before, there is some variation in the wording of the passages, but their vocabulary and themes are similar enough that they should be taken as a unit. Note that I leave *hebel* below untranslated, and I'll explain why when we discuss the meaning of this word.

> There is nothing better for the man than that he eat and drink and cause his soul to see good in his labor. Even this I saw, that it is from the hand of God, for who can eat and who can enjoy apart from him? For to the man who is pleasing before his face, he gives wisdom and knowledge and joy, but to the sinner he gives the task to gather and to collect to give to the one who is pleasing before the face of God. This also is *hebel* and a pursuit of wind.
> (Eccl 2:24–16)

> I know that there is nothing better for them than to rejoice and do good in their lifetimes. And also every man should eat, drink, and see good in his labor: it is the gift of God.
> (Eccl 3:12–13)[10]

---

10. The entire context for these verses is Eccl 3:10–15. This is the portion pertinent to the present discussion.

> And I saw that there is nothing better than that the man should rejoice in his work, for it is his portion. For who can bring him to see what will be after him?
>
> (Eccl 3:22)[11]

> Behold what I have seen: it is good and appropriate to eat, to drink, and to see good in all his labor that he labors under the sun during the few days of his life that God has given to him, for it is his portion. Also, every man to whom God has given riches and wealth and empowered him to eat from it, and to receive his portion, and to enjoy his labor: this is a gift of God.
>
> (Eccl 5:18–19)[12]

> So I commended joy because there is nothing better for the man under the sun than to eat, to drink, and to rejoice. It will join him in his toil the days of his life that God has given to him under the sun.
>
> (Eccl 8:15)[13]

> Go, eat with joy your bread and drink your wine with a happy heart, for God has already

---

11. The entire context for this verse is Eccl 3:16–22. This is the portion pertinent to the present discussion.

12. The entire context for these verses is Eccl 5:18–20 (17–19). This is the portion pertinent to the present discussion.

13. The entire context for this verse is Eccl 8:10–15. This is the portion pertinent to the present discussion.

accepted your works. At all times may your garments be white, and do not let oil be lacking upon your head. Enjoy life with the woman whom you love all the days of your *hebel* life that he has given you under the sun, all the days of your *hebel*. For it is your portion in life and in your labor that you have labored under the sun. All that your hand finds to do, do it with your strength, for there is no work or planning or knowledge or wisdom in Sheol, where you are going.
(Eccl 9:7–10)

Indeed, if a man lives many years, in all of them may he rejoice, but remember the days of darkness, that they will be many; all that comes is *hebel*. Rejoice, young man, in the days of your youth, and may your heart cheer you in the days of your youth. Walk in the way of your heart and the sight of your eyes, but know that upon all these things God will bring judgment. So remove vexation from your heart and put away evil from your body, for youth and the dawn of life are *hebel*.
(Eccl 11:8–10)

These seven passages repeat themes and vocabulary from Genesis 2:15–25 (outlined in the chart below):

And Yahweh God took the man and placed him in the garden of Eden to work it and to keep it. And Yahweh God commanded the man: "From every tree in the garden you may surely eat, but from the tree of the knowledge of good and evil you shall not eat, for in the day you eat from it, you will surely die." And Yahweh God said, "It is not good for the man to be alone. I will make for him a helper as his counterpart."

So Yahweh God formed from the ground every animal of the field and every bird of the sky, and he brought them to the man to see what he would name them. And whatever the man called a living being, that was its name. And the man named names for every livestock and bird of the air, but for the man there was not found a helper as his counterpart. So Yahweh God caused a deep sleep to fall upon the man and he slept. And he took one of his ribs and closed the flesh there. And Yahweh God built the rib that he took from the man into a woman and brought her to the man. And the man said, "This at last is bone of my bone and flesh of my flesh. She will be named 'woman' because from man she was taken."

Therefore a man leaves his father and his mother and clings to his wife and becomes one flesh. And both the man and the woman were naked and were not ashamed.

(Gen 2:15–25)

	Eccl 2:24–26	Eccl 3:10–15	Eccl 3:16–22	Eccl 5:18–20 (17–19)
Repeated terms	man/human	man/human	man/human	man/human
	good	good	good	good
	"to eat"	"to eat"		"to eat"
	God	God	God	God
Approximate synonyms	toil	toil	toil	toil (2x)

	Eccl 8:10–15	Eccl 9:7–10	Eccl 11:8–10	Gen 2:15–25
Repeated terms	man/human		man/human	man/human (9x)
	good	good	good	good (2x)
	"to eat"	"to eat"		"to eat" (4x)
	God	God	God	God (7x)
		woman		woman (4x)
Approximate synonyms	toil	toil		work
		work		

TABLE 1.5. *Allusion in the Carpe Diem Passages*

Ecclesiastes and Genesis		
Repeated themes (taking the *carpe diem* passages as a unit)	enjoy spouse	enjoy spouse
	enjoy food	enjoy food
	enjoy work	enjoy work

TABLE 1.5. Allusion in the Carpe Diem Passages (cont'd)

In Genesis 2:15, God created the man and placed him in the garden of Eden to "work it and keep it."[14] The man is then given free rein to eat from any tree in the garden, save the tree of the knowledge of good and evil (Gen 2:16). It isn't good for the man to be alone, so God creates a woman to be with him.

Life is good in the garden—people have plenty of food to eat, work to do, and company to keep. In the so-called carpe diem passages, Qohelet picks up on these key phrases to describe a life similar to what humans first experienced in the garden of Eden.

---

14. On these two terms—which in the Pentateuch are often used for service in the temple—see, among others, Allen P. Ross, *Creation and Blessing: A Guide to the Study and Exposition of the Book of Genesis* (Grand Rapids: Baker, 1988), 124–25; Umberto Cassuto, *A Commentary on the Book of Genesis: From Adam to Noah, Genesis I–VI:8*, trans. Israel Abrahams (Jerusalem: Magnes, 1961), 122–23; Walter Brueggemann, *Genesis*, Interpretation: A Bible Commentary for Teaching and Preaching (Atlanta: John Knox, 1982), 46.

The term "man" or "human" with the definite article appears in six of the carpe diem texts. "Good" is repeated in each carpe diem text. "Wife" or "woman" is found in Ecclesiastes 9:7–10. "To eat" shows up in five of the texts, and "God" is found in each of the texts.

In addition to these terms, it is notable that each passage (except Eccl 11:7–10) repeats the injunction to find enjoyment in one's work. Qohelet uses the terms "toil" and "work," which are synonymous with Genesis's "tend."

The abundance of repeated terms and approximate synonyms makes the allusion to Genesis 2:15–25 likely. Moreover, when the carpe diem texts are treated as a unit, as they often are, the correspondence in vocabulary with Genesis 2:15–25 is overwhelming (see Table 1.5 above).[15]

Qohelet's reliance on Genesis in the carpe diem passages also demonstrates the thematic overlap between these passages. God deems his creation good—with the exception of the man's loneliness, which God rectifies.

This good creation entails the man being placed in the garden where he (presumably) enjoys eating, working, and communing with his wife. These (plus

---

15. E.g., Graham Ogden, "Qohelet's Use of the 'Nothing Is Better' Form," *Journal of Biblical Literature* 98 (1979): 339–50; R. N. Whybray, "Qoheleth, Preacher of Joy," *Journal for the Study of the Old Testament* 23 (1982): 87–98; Bartholomew, *Ecclesiastes*, 80; Tremper Longman, *Ecclesiastes* (Grand Rapids: Eerdmans, 1997), 106; Daniel Fredericks, *Ecclesiastes & the Song of Songs*, Apollos Old Testament Commentary 16 (Downers Grove, IL: IVP Academic, 2010), 33.

drinking in moderation) are the precise elements that Qohelet advocates for us to enjoy in this post-sin, death-ridden, upside-down life.[16] He highlights the aspects of life that were "good" in Genesis 2 as the gifts that God gives and that we are to enjoy as God allows.

Craig Bartholomew states that these seven carpe diem passages are "the vision evoked with Eden in Gen. 2 and in the promises to the Israelites about the good land of Israel," and that they present "an alternative vision set in contradictory juxtaposition to the conclusion of *hebel* that Qohelet's epistemology leads him to."[17] The evidence indicates that Qohelet *has* singled out these particular aspects of life in order to present us with an "alternative vision" that we should seek out in the face of death.

In light of the overwhelming nature of death and the uncertainty and injustice that mark life, Qohelet urges us to return to the good that once was. Ultimately, he argues, the only good to be found in life is in capturing a part of Eden by enjoying these fleeting gifts from God.

Furthermore, he encourages this enjoyment in the most orthodox way possible: first, by proclaiming God's sovereignty over enjoyment; and second, by reminding us that we must fear and obey God (Eccl 12:13).

In sum, he uses Genesis 2:15–25 to remind us that sin is the ultimate cause for death and injustice in life, that God's gifts represent a portion of life before sin

---

16. Graham S. Ogden, *Qoheleth*, 2nd ed., Readings: A New Biblical Commentary (Sheffield: Sheffield Phoenix, 2007), 52–53.

17. Bartholomew, *Ecclesiastes*, 152.

and should therefore be enjoyed, and that God is sovereign and therefore must be feared and obeyed. We will return to these themes and their significance for the Christian life in chapter 3.

THAT WICKED HUMAN HEART

In Ecclesiastes 8:11 and 9:3, Qohelet reveals his view of the human heart: it is utterly wicked. His comments are reminiscent of two verses in Genesis (6:5; 8:21) where Yahweh makes a similar observation about humanity.[18] In Genesis 6:5, Yahweh states that he will destroy humanity (except for Noah and his family) because of its great wickedness; and in 8:21 he says that he will never again curse the ground because of the wickedness of the human heart.

The word parallels between these four passages are striking, with the repetition of "heart," "the man," and "evil." Further, "under the sun" in Ecclesiastes 9:3 and "on the earth" in Genesis 6:5 have the same basic meaning.

---

18. See Andreas Schüle, "Evil from the Heart: Qoheleth's Negative Anthropology and Its Canonical Context," in *The Language of Qohelet in Its Context: Essays in Honour of Prof. A. Schoors on the Occasion of His Seventieth Birthday*, ed. A. Berlejung and P. van Hecke, Orientalia Lovaniensia Analecta 164 (Leuven: Peeters, 2007), 168. This entire section of his essay (165–69) is instructive.

> Thus a sentence against an evil deed is not made quickly; therefore the heart of the sons of man is full in them to do evil.
>
> (Eccl 8:11)

> This is an evil in all that is done under the sun: that one fate is for all. And also the heart of the sons of men is full of evil, and foolishness is in their hearts during their lives and afterward to death.
>
> (Eccl 9:3)

> And Yahweh saw that the wickedness of man was great on the earth and every intention of the thoughts of his heart was only evil every day.
>
> (Gen 6:5)

> And Yahweh smelled the soothing aroma and Yahweh said to his heart, "Never again will I curse the ground on account of man because the intention of the heart of man is evil from his youth. And I will never again smite all living things as I did."
>
> (Gen 8:21)

In addition to the similar vocabulary in these passages, each verse speaks explicitly about the sinfulness of the human heart. Ecclesiastes 8:11 argues that, because justice is not swift, the heart is full of evil. Similarly, Qohelet laments in 9:3 that all people share the same fate—death—and that while we are alive, our hearts are full of evil.

These statements correspond to Genesis 6:5 and 8:21, in which the evilness of the human heart is of paramount importance. The primary factor in each of these four texts is that humans are full of wickedness.

	Ecclesiastes 8:11	Ecclesiastes 9:3	Genesis 6:5	Genesis 8:21
Repeated Terms	evil	evil (3x)	evil (2x)	evil
	heart	heart	heart	heart
	man/human being	man/human being	man/human being	man/human being
Approximate synonyms		under the sun	on the earth	
Syntactical features	repeated terms and approximate synonyms serve similar syntactical functions			
	repeated terms figure prominently in their contexts			
Repeated themes	evilness of the human heart			

TABLE 1.6. Allusion in Ecclesiastes 8:11; 9:3

Andreas Schüle has argued that Qohelet uses the flood narrative in Ecclesiastes 8:11 and 9:3 to support his view that the human heart is corrupt.[19] Qohelet's view clearly draws from the statements in Genesis

---

19. Schüle, "Evil from the Heart," 168.

regarding humanity's propensity to sin; however, we may also sense tension with God's statement in Genesis 8:21 that he will not punish the world in the same way.

Does Qohelet's statement that men are made to do evil because justice is not carried out swiftly (Eccl 8:11) betray his frustration with Yahweh's promise not to judge humanity now with the same method he used before? Perhaps, but Qohelet later states that Yahweh will in fact judge people, regardless of the swiftness of that judgment (Eccl 3:17; 8:12; 12:14).

Qohelet referred to Genesis 3:19 to highlight the cause of death, and here he references the flood narrative to support his theological reflections on the depth of humanity's sinfulness. Since we see that he takes his view of sin and the human condition from the author of Genesis, this points us to his reliance on Genesis's theological framework for his book of Ecclesiastes.

CONCLUSION

I enjoyed hip-hop music long before I had any idea what the artists were really saying. I benefited from listening to it because it gave voice to the anger and pain I felt. My circumstances were different from those of the hip-hop artists, to be sure, but the music still gave me a way to process and expend the emotions roiling inside of me.

Now, a few decades later, I've spent time thinking through events like the Watts riots and the beating of Rodney King; I've read the work of people like Frederick Douglass, Malcolm X, Martin Luther King, Jr., and Ida B. Wells. And I've lived—though at a distance—through more recent events like the shooting deaths of Michael Brown and Philando Castile. So when I return to the albums of N.W.A., Ice Cube, Tupac, and Eazy-E, I have a significantly deeper understanding of what they are saying and why they are saying it. And when I listen to folks like Jay-Z and Eminem, I can now bring more cultural understanding that helps me sift through and pick up on the manifold allusions these artists make in their work.

In the same way, reading Ecclesiastes benefits us even if we never see its allusions to Genesis. But when we tap into the rich cultural and literary heritage Qohelet uses here, our understanding explodes. We are then welcomed into the deep and exhilarating world of textual layering that gives insight not only into the Bible but also into how we live out the Bible today.

And this chapter is just the beginning. Next, we will look at the key word that Qohelet uses in Ecclesiastes—variously translated as "vanity," "meaningless," "absurd," and even "s***." When we set it against the background of Genesis, however, we find that it's actually a reference to Abel—the very first tragic example of a world turned upside down.

Chapter 2

ABEL AND THE MEANING OF "VANITY"

I grew up down the road from my mom's mom, Mimi. I could see her front porch from my own, and her house is where I spent most of my time as a child. I was expelled from preschool when I was around three years old for being obnoxious, so Mimi kept me while my parents worked.

We grew very close and became even closer after my dad left three years later, when I was six. Mimi became my lifeline, my rock when everything else was unsteady, and a thousand other clichés meant to help us talk about the people who matter.

Mimi—or Elsie, as her friends called her—grew a garden to feed the neighbors who couldn't afford to eat. She often called on the elderly folks in our neighborhood, dragging me along with her. She took me to yard sales and taught me how to put together puzzles, and together we curated an enormous stamp collection.

Mimi took me to church, where I eagerly listened to Brother Steele, even though I was confused when he told us that we should believe gossip and that we should also *not* believe gossip.

Mimi enjoyed explaining that *gossip* and *gospel* are two very different words.

About five years after my dad left, I came home from Vacation Bible School, walked into her house, and immediately spotted a piece of gauze wrapped around her arm. "My lymphoma's back," was the only thing I could make out as she collapsed, crying, into my aunt's arms.

But those words had no meaning for me. All I could think was, "That cut must really hurt."

It was the second time she'd had cancer. After Mimi started chemo and her hair was falling out, we sat in her car as she sang "Amazing Grace" with tears streaming down her face.

I don't know that I've ever been angrier or more confused than I was in that moment.

Grace!? You're dying, Mimi!

It wasn't long after that the cancer won. Death had *not* lost its sting—at least not for a preteen boy who'd already lost his dad.

It didn't seem right or fair or in any way representative of the God my grandmother sang about. And it took a lot of years to untangle the knot of suffering, death, and injustice that wrapped itself around my heart.

The book of Ecclesiastes turned out to be a key conversation partner for me in that effort, and specifically the themes of Ecclesiastes we'll look at in this chapter.

ABEL AND *HEBEL*

In the last chapter, we examined the many passages in Ecclesiastes that allude to Genesis, which would have brought Genesis to the minds of Qohelet's original readers. As we saw, these passages create a Genesis-shaped framework for reading the entire book of Ecclesiastes.

One key allusion that we didn't look at yet, however, is the word *Abel*. Of course, we know this as the name of the murdered son from Genesis 4—but it's also a key word that marks nearly every chapter of Ecclesiastes.

Reading *hebel* in Ecclesiastes as a reference to *Abel* in Genesis is far from a slam-dunk case. It's only one word, and the thematic overlap requires some biblical-theological maneuvering with which some take issue. Nevertheless, I think the many allusions to Genesis in Ecclesiastes create an interpretive context in which the term *hebel* naturally calls to our minds the life of Abel—at the very least because in Hebrew, Abel's name is *Hebel*. In the English translation it becomes "Abel," but the spelling is exactly the same in Genesis as in Ecclesiastes.

Below, we'll see below how Abel's life illustrates Ecclesiastes in living color. So, we can understand more fully the book of Ecclesiastes—and therefore understand how in the world we are supposed to live in this sin-ridden, upside-down world—if we investigate how Qohelet uses *hebel* as a reference to Abel the person.

Let's start by looking at how *hebel* is used outside of Ecclesiastes to lay a foundation for how we should understand its use within Ecclesiastes, then move on to something called "retribution theology," and finally reflect on what *hebel* means in Ecclesiastes in light of the Cain and Abel narrative.

WHAT DOES *HEBEL* MEAN?

The word *hebel* appears in the Old Testament eighty-six times.[20] It is used almost entirely in a metaphorical sense, with translations such as "vanity," "meaningless," and "absurd," though some passages use its concrete (or dictionary) meaning: "vapor" or "breath" (e.g., Ps 62:10).

In some contexts, this metaphorical use refers to idolatry; while in others, it refers to the brevity of human life, the emptiness of words, or the fleetingness of ill-gotten wealth.

Regardless of the specific context in which *hebel* appears, it almost exclusively refers to some aspect of either idols or humans, often in contrast to God. Most importantly, *hebel* often describes things that do not produce their intended results.

---

20. Gen 4:2 (2x), 4 (2x), 8 (2x), 9, 25; Deut 32:21; 1 Kgs 16:13, 26; 2 Kgs 17:15 (2x); Job 7:16; 9:29; 21:34; 27:12 (2x); 35:16; Pss 31:7; 39:6, 7, 12; 62:10 (2x), 11; 78:33; 94:11; 144:4; Prov 13:11; 21:6; 31:30; Eccl 1:2 (5x), 14; 2:1, 11, 15, 17, 19, 21, 23, 26; 3:19; 4:4, 7, 8, 16; 5:6, 9; 6:2, 4, 9, 11, 12; 7:6, 15; 8:10, 14 (2x); 9:9 (2x); 11:8; 11:10; 12:8 (3x); Isa 30:7; 49:4; 57:13; Jer 2:5 (2x); 8:19; 10:3, 8, 15; 14:22; 16:19; 23:16; 51:18; Lam 4:17; Jonah 2:9; Zech 10:2.

For example: neither idols nor Egypt can save Israel; "vain" talk cannot comfort; inappropriately gained wealth doesn't provide security; death levels all; and righteousness does not always prove innocence, as Job's heartrending story shows us. The following survey organizes *hebel* around its referent—that is, what it symbolizes.

Idolatry

Outside of Ecclesiastes, *hebel* most often appears in reference to idolatry, either to idols themselves or to the result of worshiping idols. In the second instance, it is used to say that idolaters become like their idols: nothing, inconsequential, vaporous.

In such cases, the reference to *hebel* is set in contrast with Yahweh and is often accompanied by language that describes the provocation of the Lord's anger against idolatry (e.g., Deut 32:21; 1 Kgs 16:13, 26; 2 Kgs 17:15 [2x]; Jer 2:5; 8:19).

This use of *hebel* is most common in the prophetic books, particularly Jeremiah (2:5; 8:19; 10:3, 8, 15; 16:19; 51:18). Jonah (2:8) and Zechariah (10:2) also use *hebel* to talk about idolatry. Isaiah 57:13 uses *hebel* to refer to the fleetingness of idols, stating that they can be blown away by a "breath" and that a "vapor" (*hebel*) will carry them off.[21]

---

21. See Joseph Blenkinsopp, *Isaiah 56–66*, Anchor Bible 19 (New York: Doubleday, 2003), 153. Stephen J. Andrews (personal correspondence, October 2014) suggested that the use of *hebel*

Outside of the prophetic books, *hebel* refers to idols in Psalm 31:6: "I hate those who are devoted to *worthless* idols, but as for me, I trust in Yahweh."

In Proverbs 31, the poem of the valiant woman, *hebel* appears again, this time in reference to beauty. In this passage, most English translations render *hebel* as "fleeting" to communicate the transient nature of beauty. For example, the Christian Standard Bible says, "Charm is deceptive and beauty is *fleeting*" (Prov 31:30; see also NLT, CEB, NIV, NET, NKJV).

However, *hebel* is parallel to another Hebrew word that means "falsehood" or "deceptive." Further, the next line highlights what really matters for this "valiant woman": "a woman who fears the LORD will be praised."[22] In context, then, *hebel* refers *not* to the fleetingness of beauty but rather to its inherent deceitfulness, as the author likewise describes "charm." Like idols, beauty and charm are untrustworthy because they do not make good on their promises. This untrustworthiness of outward appearance contrasts with the person who fears Yahweh—an inward disposition that by its nature is not as obvious as charm and beauty or the external features of a person.

Isaiah 30:7 also uses *hebel* in the context of idolatry; that is, looking to something other than God for

---

in this context to refer to idols being blown away is a possible instance of paronomasia (that is, a play on words or a pun).

22. See John A. Kitchen, *Proverbs*, Mentor Commentary (Ross-Shire, Scotland: Mentor, 2006), 722; Roland E. Murphy, *Proverbs*, Word Biblical Commentary 22 (Nashville: Thomas Nelson, 1998), 248. Murphy notes that the most important aspect of this verse is the second cola, which highlights the fear of Yahweh.

what only God can do (see also Lam 4:7). In this passage, Israel is looking to Egypt, rather than to the Lord, for help.[23] Though the context is slightly different from out-and-out idolatry, the takeaway remains the same: No one but Yahweh is capable to act on Israel's behalf.

Human Life

Hebel is also used to describe human life in its denotative sense of "breath" or "vapor," which is sometimes expanded to the concept of "brevity" or "transience."

This usage can be seen in Psalm 39, where the psalmist speaks of the fleeting nature of his life (see Pss 39:6–7, 12; 78:33; 94:11; 144:4).[24]

Hebel is used this way once in Job (7:16), where Job states that he "will not live forever" because his "days are a *breath*" (CSB).

Words

Hebel sometimes refers to the "emptiness" or "nothingness" of words, such as in Job 21:34 and 35:16, and possibly in Isaiah 49:4.

In Job 21:34, he accuses his friends of comforting him with *hebel*; that is, their words are "empty" or "nothing" because they do not actually do what they

---

23. The second half of Isa 30:7 has presented many difficulties for translators. For an overview of the issues, see Aron Pinker, "Isaiah 30,7b," *Biblische Notizen* 136 (2008): 31–44.

24. When *hebel* is used in this sense, its surrounding context often includes terms such as *yom* ("day"; e.g., Pss 39:6, 7, 12; 78:33; 144:4) to indicate that the author is referring to a span of time.

are meant to do, which is comfort (or even convince!) Job. Similarly, in 35:16, Elihu accuses Job of speaking words that amount to "nothing," words that fail in their purpose of exonerating Job.

In Isaiah 49:4, the prophet complains that "*hebel* I spent my strength." Here, Isaiah appears to be complaining that his strength has been spent for "nothing." His words have come to naught, or *hebel*, in that they have not produced the intended result of repentance. Words, then, are *hebel* when they do not accomplish their intended purpose.

Wealth

Proverbs employs *hebel* twice in the context of wealth. Proverbs 13:11 contrasts *hebel* with hard work, stating that wealth gained from *hebel* will diminish, but wealth gained from working hard will increase. While some see this passage as referring to the transience of ill-gotten wealth, the verse's parallelism indicates that *hebel* here is actually contrasted with hard work.

Thus the word appears to mean something along the lines of "deception," similar to how it is used in contexts that address idolatry—ill-gotten wealth does not do what it is supposed to do. Rather than providing peace and security, it passes through one's fingers and is therefore *hebel*.[25] Psalm 62:10 and Proverbs 21:6 similarly use *hebel* to describe ill-gained wealth.

---

25. Bruce K. Waltke, *Proverbs 1–15*, New International Commentary on the Old Testament (Grand Rapids: Eerdmans, 2004), 561.

Unexpected Results

Finally, in 9:29, Job uses *hebel* to refer to a broken relationship between actions and their expected consequences. He states, "I am condemned. Why then do I toil with *hebel*?"

Throughout the book of Job, the person Job protests his suffering because he is *innocent*. He's done nothing to deserve the suffering he is experiencing. His protests of innocence, though, do nothing to stop the deluge of suffering. He is condemned, and so he wonders why he labors "with *hebel*," or "in a way that does not produce the expected results." His righteous life and protestations of innocence should have relieved his suffering, but neither is effective, neither produces the intended results.

SO, AGAIN, WHAT DOES *HEBEL* MEAN?

Now we return to the initial question: What in the world does *hebel* mean? Context determines meaning, and words are used in different ways in different contexts. For example, my youngest son just learned—gleefully—that "bat" can refer both to a black, winged creature that turns people into vampires (at least in his imagination!) and also to a wooden stick used to strike a ball.

Those are homonyms of course, so a better illustration might be the word *bread*, which can refer to all sorts of things made of the basic ingredients of flour, sugar, water, and sometimes yeast. A donut is not a dinner roll, but both are "bread." Thus "Pass me the bread" said at dinner would refer to an altogether different thing than it would at breakfast; and the word's meaning is even more different when someone says, "Let's get this bread!"—that is, money. Same word, different meanings. Context determines what we're talking about.

Broadly speaking, based on the discussion above, we can categorize *hebel* as a word with both metaphorical and concrete meanings. Its concrete meaning is "breath" or "vapor," which is then expanded metaphorically to refer to basically two different sorts of things:

- Things that do not last
- Things that do not produce their intended results; that is, a disconnect between actions and their rewards, or the breakdown of the retribution principle.

The story of Abel (*Hebel* in Hebrew) beautifully illustrates both aspects of this word, and I think that tragic story is what Qohelet wants us to consider when we read the word *hebel* in his book.

RETRIBUTION THEOLOGY IN THE LIFE OF ABEL

I am going to assume that you're familiar with the story of Cain and Abel, in which the wicked Cain refuses to conquer the sin that is "crouching at the door" (Gen 4:7). Instead, he vents his anger and embarrassment over God's rebuke by murdering his brother. The Bible is clear that Abel did nothing to deserve Cain's wrath, in which Cain persisted despite God's pleading with him to do right and turn back to God. Abel was righteous. Cain was not. Abel the righteous, however, was murdered by Cain the unrighteous.

In order to fully grasp what's going on in this story—particularly, to understand the role it plays in Ecclesiastes—we need to fast-forward just a bit in the narrative of the Bible.

The Cain and Abel story is not just about jealousy and murder and improper worship. It's also about the failure of actions to produce their expected outcomes; that is, the failure of something scholars call "retribution theology." We can see this theology most clearly in places like Deuteronomy and Job, where we now turn before revisiting the two brothers.

The covenant God made with Israel when he brought them out of Egypt is alternately called the Deuteronomic covenant, the Mosaic covenant, the Sinaitic covenant, and the old covenant. This covenant is grounded in Yahweh's choice of Israel, which Deuteronomy traces back to the covenant relationship between Yahweh and Abraham, Isaac, and Jacob (Deut 1:8).

Throughout Deuteronomy, the Lord reminds Israel that the basis of their relationship is Yahweh's grace—not their own merit. However, as with the rest of the Bible (even the New Testament), human actions matter. In the Deuteronomic covenant, Israel's obedience or disobedience to Yahweh mattered both in the people's relationship with Yahweh and their way of life—much like the way my children's relationship with me and their way of life is impacted by whether they're "actin' right," as we say where I'm from.

Because God loves his people and wants to live in a good relationship with them, Deuteronomy outlines the stipulations of this covenant and the results of either keeping or failing to keep these stipulations. Again, this is similar to how good parents set boundaries, establish consequences both good and bad, and explain all of this to their children.

Although these boundaries and subsequent consequences are laced throughout Deuteronomy, we'll focus on just a few passages here. Deuteronomy 7:11–15 delineates the blessings contingent on Israel's obedience to God. If the people obey the commands and statutes of Yahweh, then he will give them descendants, abundant crops and herds, and good health. The passage goes on to assure the Israelites that they will possess the land of their enemies, which represents the fulfillment of Yahweh's promise to Abraham in Genesis 22.[26]

The path to these blessings is straightforward: obedience to the covenant requirements. The context also shows that blessing comes from Yahweh because of his love and faithfulness to Israel's ancestors.

Thus the Bible holds in tension human obedience and God's grace: obedience to the covenant is para-

---

26. See J. G. McConville, *Deuteronomy*, Apollos Old Testament Commentary (Downers Grove, IL: IVP Academic, 2002), 201.

mount, but Yahweh's grace is ultimately responsible for their blessing.

Deuteronomy 24:17–22 provides another example of the relationship between God's grace and Israel's responsibility to keep the covenant requirements. In this passage, Israel is commanded to relate to the underprivileged in society with justice and fairness. The rationale given for their treatment of the underprivileged is twofold:

1. Yahweh redeemed Israel from slavery in Egypt, so that

2. Yahweh might bless them.

Again, blessing comes from obedience, but God's grace is fully responsible for blessings. Despite what many may think, God is not a cosmic candy machine where you can drop in a quarter to get out whatever you want.[27]

In Deuteronomy 30:11–20, Moses assures the Israelites that these commandments can be obeyed, for they are near to them in their hearts (vv. 11–14). The people cannot charge God with making the conditions of blessing too difficult.

This passage also explains what blessing consists of: descendants, reputation, physical provision—both sustenance and victory over enemies—land, and long life.

---

27. One of my former graduate school professors, Blake Hearson, often used this illustration in his lectures.

In sum, Deuteronomy shows that blessing is contingent on obedience to the covenant *and* streams from Yahweh's grace.

Other biblical books confirm this basic understanding of the relationship between actions and consequence: obedience results in blessing, and disobedience results in curses.

For example, Proverbs argues that righteous living leads to being blessed and unrighteous living leads to being cursed. Though Proverbs does not present a rigid retribution theology, it certainly presents a worldview governed by the principles of retribution theology.

The book of Job also contains the basic formulation that actions and their results should have a predictable relationship, but Job introduces another piece to this puzzle. As a righteous person, he should not suffer the curses brought upon him, and that's why his friends are so adamant that he must have sinned: their theological system doesn't allow for a righteous sufferer.

Let's press pause briefly on this conversation and keep it in the back of our minds as we look again at what is going on in the first few chapters of Genesis—and why Qohelet picks up on this story as a way to wrestle with retribution theology in particular.

The basic formulation of retribution theology—obedience results in blessing while disobedience results in curses—was operative in the first few chapters of Genesis.

For example, in Genesis 3 disobedience resulted in being cursed. Adam and Eve suffered the consequences of their sin—death, separation from God, pain, and strenuous work (vv. 14–19). This pattern of sin and punishment, however, does not hold true for the Cain and Abel narrative.

As we know, Abel offered an acceptable sacrifice to Yahweh and Cain did not. After Yahweh rejected Cain's sacrifice, he warned an angry Cain that sin was ready to devour him, and he admonished Cain to "overtake" sin before it consumed him. Cain failed to heed this warning and instead murdered his brother.

Although Yahweh cursed him (Gen 4:11–12), Cain protested that the punishment was too severe. In response, Yahweh mitigated the curse by placing on Cain a sign of protection (4:13–15). His life was prolonged, he had many descendants, and he built a city (4:17). *Cain, "who belonged to the evil one"* (1 John 3:12 NIV), *received the blessings for obedience* (outlined later in Deuteronomy; see esp. 7:11–15; 28:1–14; 30:11–20).[28]

On the other hand, *"righteous Abel"* (as Jesus referred to him in Matt 23:35) *suffered the consequences of disobedience* (also outlined in Deuteronomy; see esp. 28:15–68). His life was cut short, ostensibly leaving him

---

28. This is not meant to imply that Cain received *no* punishment, but that the punishment was not as severe as would be expected or deserved. J. McKeown (*Genesis*, The Two Horizons Old Testament Commentary [Grand Rapids: Eerdmans, 2008], 42) states, "Cain's complaint is not dismissed, and he is reassured that whoever kills him will suffer sevenfold vengeance. Yahweh places a mysterious sign or mark on Cain to protect his life," but "whereas blessing had fostered harmony, cursing breeds separation and alienation."

with no children, no heritage, and no material wealth. The one-to-one relationship between disobedience and curses or obedience and blessing had been reversed.

At this point, the world has clearly been turned upside down. The righteous suffer and the unrighteous prosper.

This brief, early narrative of the first time when the expected relationship between actions and consequences breaks down is one of the key ways in which *hebel* is used in the Old Testament.

Centuries later, Qohelet presents Abel as the embodiment of human tragedy, which everyone since—including us today—has experienced in one way or another.

ABEL IN ECCLESIASTES

Ecclesiastes 1:2 loudly proclaims that everything is *hebel*—something Qohelet's readers would remember from the Cain and Abel (*Hebel*) narrative. In the Old Testament, names often reveal some aspect of a person's character, or as scholar Tremper Longman says, "Naming captures the essential nature of a person or thing."[29] For example, Cain was "gotten" by Eve (Gen 4:1), and Abraham is the "father of a multitude" (Gen 17:5).

The same holds true for Abel. The nonmetaphorical meaning of his name is "breath" or "vapor," which by its nature is ephemeral and transient.[30] Jacques

---

29. Longman, *Ecclesiastes*, 177.
30. K. Seybold, "*Hebel*," *Theological Dictionary of the Old Testament* 3:315. See also *HALOT*, 236–37.

Ellul states that Abel was so named for this very reason. Even though he is the righteous character in the narrative, Cain cuts short Abel's life.[31] Abel is thus the embodiment of transience.

Joseph Blenkinsopp also argues that Abel's name presupposes his murder at the hands of his brother, indicating that Abel is "breath"—a theme Qohelet develops by commenting on the transience of all humans (for example, Eccl 3:19–20).[32] This allusion continues throughout the book.

By using *hebel* as the leitmotif, Qohelet expands this theme of transience and injustice introduced in Genesis 4: Everyone and everything in life is subject to the reversal that Abel experienced.[33]

However, it seems more is at work in Qohelet's writing than simply the matter of transience. He also uses *hebel* as a symbol to discuss how human life has mirrored the tragedy of Abel since the day Cain murdered him.

---

31. Jacques Ellul, *Reason for Being: A Meditation on Ecclesiastes* (Grand Rapids: Eerdmans, 1990), 50.

32. Joseph Blenkinsopp, *Creation, Un-Creation, Re-Creation: A Discursive Commentary on Genesis 1–11* (London: T&T Clark, 2011), 84–85. See also Charles C. Forman, "Koheleth's Use of Genesis," *Journal of Semitic Studies* 5, no. 3 (1960): 258.

33. See Daniel Fredericks, *Coping with Transience* (Sheffield: JSOT Press, 1993), 1–32. Note also Robert Alter (*The Wisdom Books: Job, Proverbs, and Ecclesiastes: A Translation with Commentary* [New York: Norton, 2010], 346), who prefers the word *breath* because "*Hevel*, 'breath' or 'vapor,' is something utterly insubstantial and transient, and in this book suggests futility, ephemerality, and also as Fox argues, the absurdity of existence."

Instead of explicitly stating his assessment of something gone wrong, Qohelet leaves it to us to decide which aspect of Abel story he's talking about: transience, the broken relationship between actions and rewards, the injustice suffered, the inability to attain lasting value—all of which are summed up in the failure of the retribution principle in Abel's case.

In Ecclesiastes 1:14, Qohelet states that he has seen all the works done under the sun and that they are all *hebel* and a pursuit of wind. By making *hebel* parallel with pursuing wind, Qohelet points to the inability of all people, like Abel, to grasp anything with lasting value. The obedient *should* experience tangible blessings that add value to their lives. For Qohelet, however, the one-to-one correspondence between actions and rewards has been blown away, so now trying to attain anything of lasting value is like trying to grasp the wind.

In 2:15, Qohelet laments that the wise and foolish are alike in their end: they all die. No one escapes Abel's fate—the culmination of the curses that God pronounced after the fall.[34] We see this, of course, in Abel. The anticipated relationship between actions and rewards makes no sense. Fool or wise—both are subject to the same fate.

In 3:19, Qohelet says that "man has no advantage over the beasts, for all are *hebel*." We all share the same

---

34. William H. U. Anderson, "The Curse of Work in Qoheleth: An Exposé of Genesis 3:17–19 in Ecclesiastes," *Evangelical Quarterly* 70 (1998): 99–113.

breath of life and the same fate of death. This is another way he elaborates on the theme of transience first introduced in Genesis 4. Abel's life was fleeting, and so is everything else—human and animal alike.

Similarly, the "Royal Experiment"[35] of Ecclesiastes 2 finds that everything in life is ephemeral, lacking any lasting value, and that our only recourse is to enjoy the gifts of God: eating, drinking, a spouse, and pleasurable toil, which are themselves also transient (2:24–25).

Another aspect of Abel's life that Qohelet discusses is the disconnect between hard work and the fruit of our labor. For example, he states in 4:4,

> And I myself saw all the toil and all the skill of work, that this is from the envy of a man of his fellow. This also is *hebel*, and a pursuit of wind.[36]

Qohelet indicates that labor and work—the effort to acquire—result from envying others. Instead of working as a way to fulfill God's command to work and the blessing it brings to us and those around us, Qohelet

---

35. Thomas Krüger, *Qoheleth* (Minneapolis: Fortress, 2001), 45.

36. This passage could also refer to the envy that Cain felt as a result of Yahweh's accepting Abel's offering while rejecting his own, which resulted in Cain's acquisition of wealth and progeny while Abel suffered from lack of both. See Radiša Antic, "Cain, Abel, Seth and the Meaning of Human Life as Portrayed in the Books of Genesis and Ecclesiastes," *Andrews University Seminary Studies* 44 (2006): 203–11.

tells us that hard work comes from envy. The desire to keep up with the Joneses, not the desire to contribute meaningfully to society, drives work in the post-fall, upside-down world we inhabit. The right order of the world is reversed.

In 4:8, we can see how the person who has no children resembles Abel:

> And for whom am I laboring and depriving
> myself from the good?
> This also is *hebel* and an evil task.

This person works tirelessly to establish wealth and honor, yet he does not receive the blessing of descendants to inherit his wealth. This is a grievous wrong since wealth represents blessing from Yahweh, a "normal reward for righteous living."[37] Yahweh, however, has withheld the blessing of progeny. Since he obtained the blessing of wealth, shouldn't he also experience the blessing of children? The former without the latter is an "evil" thing.

Finally, Qohelet states in 8:14,

> There is *hebel* that is done upon the earth: that there are righteous to whom it happens according to the deeds of the wicked, and there are wicked to whom it happens according to the deeds of the righteous. I said that this also is *hebel*.

---

37. Robert Ellis, "Amos Economics," *Review and Expositor* 107 (2010): 463–79. See also Deut 7:11–15.

This passage is Ecclesiastes's most explicit reference to the reversal of the expected order of life. As in the Cain and Abel narrative, so in the rest of life, sometimes the disobedient receive blessing while the obedient receive curses.[38] As we all are painfully aware, the world is often turned upside down, which is what Qohelet asks us to remember when he says,

"Abel of Abels, everything is Abel."

CONCLUSION

As I mentioned at the outset of this chapter, the linguistic overlap between the use of *hebel* in Ecclesiastes and its use in Genesis is only this one term. However, *hebel* is a rare word in the Old Testament, occurring only eighty-six times, with thirty-eight of those occurrences in Ecclesiastes and eight of them in Genesis 4.

The clustering of the term in Ecclesiastes indicates its prominence for the book as a whole, and its use in Genesis 4, where it names one of the narrative's main characters, indicates its prominence there. The bulk of the evidence for Qohelet's use of *hebel* as an intentional allusion to Genesis 4 rests on Qohelet's overall use of Genesis and the thematic correspondences between Genesis 4 and Ecclesiastes.

---

38. Longman (*Ecclesiastes*, 131) makes a similar observation about Eccl 3:22 but argues that Qohelet is uncertain whether there will *ever* be justice.

All that said, if we read *hebel* in Ecclesiastes as a reference to Abel's life, then the implications for how we understand "the Bible's strangest book"[39] are enormous.

First, reading the book as an examination of the "Abelness" of life (when the relationship between actions and expected results is turned upside down) helps us see that Ecclesiastes is not the rumblings of a discontented sage. Rather, it's a book written from the wrestling of a faithful follower of God.

Second, if Qohelet is indeed using *hebel* as a symbol to refer to Abel's life—and all that went wrong in it—then Ecclesiastes is not at all about the "meaninglessness" or "vanity" of life. Rather, it's a book that guides us through the vagaries of life in this fallen world, offering the solution for how to navigate such a dark and twisted place.

> *The solution is to be faithfully obedient to God and enjoy his gifts.*

Taken together, these two implications—wrestling with life and offering the solution—mean that this ancient book is not only relevant for Qohelet's ancient audience but for us as well. It is for *every* human struggling to figure out what it means to live and to follow God in a world turned upside down. We will look more at this next.

---

39. Crenshaw, *Ecclesiastes*, 23.

Chapter 3

FROM HERE, WHERE? FEAR GOD AND ENJOY HIS GIFTS

"Your daddy left."

That's what my mom said to me the first time I lost my dad. As a six-year-old boy, I couldn't possibly understand all that meant, so I've spent the decades since then trying to sort it out. With every major milestone in my life, I've had to process it anew: high school graduation, college graduation, marriage, seeing my first child for the first time. "Your daddy left" tinged all those moments with gray.

"Your daddy died."

That's what my stepmom said to me the second time I lost my dad. I stood up from the table at the coffee shop, hung up the phone, and walked a few blocks to a bar. I'd spend the next several days in a drunken stupor until I could muster the courage to face what it meant to be left a second time by a man I hardly knew.

He was sixty, and his third heart attack had finally been too much.

His last words to me, spoken on Christmas night from two thousand miles away, had been, "I miss you, Son." I didn't respond. Now that I know the longing of a father for his kids, it seemed like a fitting end to our relationship.

"Your daddy molested me."

Those were the words I heard when I lost my dad for the third time. I have faint memories of hearing that sort of thing about him before, but I had always sloughed it off as impossible. Now, hearing it straight from the mouth of a person I loved and trusted, I couldn't avoid the truth of it. I stood in my concrete-floored makeshift office and felt all the good things that I'd held onto about my dad slipping through my grip.

The infrequent times I was around him, he seemed good with children, fun, and always full of laughs. You felt special when you were with him—like you were the only person in the whole world. Looking back, I can see the signs of grooming.

Losing your dad is hard. Losing him three times approaches catastrophic.

Like my dad, Mimi was sixty when she died. I've always tended to set the two of them side-by-side in my mind, comparing their lives and their deaths. It's never sat right with me that a serial adulterer, sexual abuser, and alcoholic would get the same number of years on planet Earth as the woman who so faithfully and tangibly loved me. Ecclesiastes answered that conundrum for me:

It's because life is turned upside down.

Life is marked by Abel, the first righteous person who reaped the harvest of the wicked (and, as Hebrews tells us, the approval of God). Ecclesiastes gives a paradigm for processing the injustice and pain we experience; it shows us that our experiences are not all that unique; and it gives us language for expressing the truth of what we see around us.

But Ecclesiastes doesn't leave us with only an acknowledgment that things aren't the way they should be. If it did, that would be okay. Sometimes we just need someone to acknowledge our pain, like the sixty-five-year-old man in the bar who grasped my hand that day I learned about my dad's death and said to me, "Losing your dad is hard."

Praise the Lord, though, Ecclesiastes doesn't leave us with only that stark acknowledgment. It presses forward, further into our pain, anger, and disillusionment, and it gives us two tools to navigate a world turned upside down: fearing God and enjoying his gifts.

FEAR GOD AND KEEP HIS COMMANDMENTS

The book of Ecclesiastes ends with the key for interpreting the entire book. It reads,

> The end of the matter; all has been heard. Fear God and keep his commandments, for this is the whole duty of man. For God will bring every deed into judgment, with every secret thing, whether good or evil.
>
> (Eccl 12:13–14 ESV)

In light of everything the author wrestled with over the previous twelve chapters, his parting words tell us to "fear God and keep his commandments, for this is the whole duty of man." Given that this is his last word to us, we should take careful note of what he is saying and what it might mean for how we understand and apply the book as a whole. In this section, we will therefore do just that: first, examine the phrase "this is the whole duty of man," and then discuss what it means to "fear God" and how that helps us understand the rest of the book.

The Whole Duty of Man?

Modern translations differ quite a bit in how they render this phrase, with variations including "this is for all humanity" (CSB), "this applies to every person" (NASB), "this is the duty of all mankind" (NIV), "this is man's all" (NKJV), "this is the whole duty of man" (ESV; see also NET), and "this is everyone's duty" (NLT).

The translations differ from one another because they struggle with how to communicate the meaning of a difficult phrase in Hebrew that reads woodenly, "for this is all of humanity." These translations are not altogether wrong, for they capture at least part of what Qohelet is trying to say. However, we could better translate the phrase as "the whole of humanity," or even "what it means to be a human," which the NKJV comes close to. This translation is more theologically consistent with the rest of Ecclesiastes, which is concerned with navigating the inconsistencies of a post-fall world.

The book's final summation of this life, then, is not that the whole *duty* or *responsibility* of humans is to fear God and keep his commandments—though that's included. Rather, the point is that the very essence of being human is to fear God and keep his commands. *That* is what it means to be a human, and that is the lens through which we should read the rest of the book.

Most of us understand the idea of keeping God's commands, especially those of us who grew up in religious contexts that emphasized rule-following as a means of earning (or staying in) God's favor. We will get to that discussion in just a bit, but first let's think about what it means to "fear God." Is Qohelet telling us to cower before our Almighty Maker?

Yes and no; but in my estimation, mostly no.

What Is the "Fear of God"?

In an American context, "fear" carries a few different connotations that are generally unhelpful for understanding the way the word is used in the Old Testament to describe our posture toward and relationship with God. We talk about being afraid of things like horror movies (I couldn't sleep for weeks after watching the film *Signs*). The title of the 1990s TV series *Are You Afraid of the Dark?* captures this usage of "fear" quite well.

We also use the term to describe our feelings toward something like failure. Most people rightly have an aversion to not succeeding, and they may even avoid good opportunities because they are "afraid to fail."

Neither of these really gets at what the Old Testament is talking about, however, when it says that we should "fear God."

A third way we use the term "fear" is to describe an emotional or a physiological response: fight-flight-freeze. A fearful situation may cause us to, for example, run for safety in the face of harm or death. This is the fear portrayed in horror films when people run from (or cower before) ax murderers. But this type of fear can also be good for us; it's something that prevents us from harming ourselves, like touching a hot stove. And at its heartbreaking extreme, this is how the abused view their abuser—with fear. In its healthiest iteration, however, it gets at one part of the fear the Old Testament talks about.

Let me explain by way of a story.

When I was a young child, my dad told me not to go into the kitchen. He didn't offer any further explanation, though I doubt it would have mattered anyway. So, of course, I did exactly what any kid would do: I marched straight into the kitchen, and soon my feet were bleeding all over the place. It turns out my dad didn't want me to go into the kitchen because someone had dropped a glass, covering the floor with shards. He set me on the counter, pulled the glass out of my feet, bandaged me up, and gave me a spanking (or a whoopin' if you're from Arkansas like me).

I learned that day that:

1. my dad gave me commands for my own good, and

2. he would enforce obedience to those commands.

It instilled in me a healthy fear of getting a spanking (or having my feet cut up) that in turn caused me to do what my dad said. (Note: I'm not advocating corporal punishment; I share this only by way of illustration.) Obeying my dad, at least at that point in my life, was based on an understanding that he would punish disobedience *and* that he had my own good in mind. In short, he loved me by giving and enforcing instructions that would keep me from harm.

All illustrations break down at some point, and this one is no exception, since later my healthy fear of my dad would warp into the extreme that I mentioned above when I experienced deep and lasting pain at his hands. But this lesson still helps me understand what Qohelet is talking about when he says that fearing God is "the whole of humanity."

Fearing God, in short, means obeying God (the second part of Qohelet's admonition) because we know that:

1. God gives commands for our good because he is our Father and,

2. as our Father, God can and will issue consequences for disobedience.

Although we don't typically struggle to believe the second part of this equation, the first part may take some convincing—especially for those who grew up in a broken or abusive home and those who have lived in fear of someone.

Grounded in Covenant Relationship

Let's backtrack just a little to discuss how the ancient Israelites—and us today—can be sure about the first point: God gives commands for our good because he is our Father. We could move directly to the New Testament concept of our adoption as children by way of the new covenant established in Christ's life, death, and resurrection. That imagery of adoption, though, has its roots in how people in the Old Testament society related to one another. So, to demonstrate how the original readers of the Old Testament would have understood God as their Father, and thus how fearing God is grounded in that parent-child relationship, we need to look at how Israelite culture operated—in particular, the concept of covenant relationship.

In Israelite culture, and in the broader ancient Near East, one person's responsibility to another was determined by blood relationships. My responsibility to my son is greater than my responsibility to the kid who lives down the street. In order to create familial responsibility between unrelated people—such that my responsibility for my son would be the same as my responsibility for the kid down the street—a familial relationship has to be created. Today, the primary way this is done is through adoption and marriage; these two processes create a familial relationship where none existed before. For example, my middle son is adopted. He now has a birth certificate that lists me as his father, includes my hometown, and has on it the last name he inherited from me. He is fully and completely a Meek boy, even though I didn't meet him until he was six months old. I'm his father, forever and always, and he has the same rights and responsibilities as my biological children.

In the Old Testament culture, creating a familial relationship like the one between me and my middle son was done through a covenant. There were two basic types of covenants in the ancient Near East that laid out guidelines for unrelated parties who were going to become family: the suzerain-vassal treaty and the parity treaty. The latter created "brothers" out of two equal parties, much like modern-day treaties between nations with roughly equal power. That need not concern us here. The former, though, is particularly important for understanding how the fear of God is bound up in the parent-child relationship.

In the book of Exodus, we read about God's (partial) fulfillment of his promise to Abraham, Isaac, and Jacob to make a great nation out of Israel. More importantly for our study in Ecclesiastes, the establishment of Israel as God's people involved the creation of a familial relationship between God and his people through a covenant, such that God became Israel's Father and Israel his child.

Having rescued his people from slavery in Egypt, he led them through the wilderness and then appeared to Moses at Mount Sinai, where he ratified a covenant with them. This covenant mirrors what is known as the suzerain-vassal treaty, a common ancient Near Eastern formula in which a greater party (the suzerain) makes certain commitments to a lesser party (the vassal) who in turn makes certain commitments to the suzerain.

The suzerain-vassal treaty, or covenant, contains several distinct features, including identification of the suzerain, a discussion of the previous relationship between the parties, covenant stipulations (i.e., commands), provisions for periodic reading and safekeeping of the covenant, witnesses to the covenant, and blessings and curses for faithfulness or unfaithfulness to the covenant. All these markers are present in the covenant God made with his people at Sinai, which is recorded in Exodus and Deuteronomy.

- Exodus 20:2 identifies the Lord as the suzerain (or greater party) and reminds the Israelites of the Lord's relationship with them (he rescued them from Egypt).

- Exodus 20:3–17 records the covenant stipulations.
- Exodus 24:7 makes provision for the safekeeping and reading of the covenant.
- Deuteronomy 4:26 calls heaven and earth as witnesses to the covenant.
- Deuteronomy 27–28 contains a long list of blessings for obedience and curses for disobedience.

In short, at Sinai, God established a suzerain-vassal covenant with the people of Israel, in which God would become the Lord and "Father" of Israel and they would owe him "consummate loyalty."[40]

When God made a covenant with Israel, he became their Father. As the Lord's children, Israel was expected to obey him—or as Ecclesiastes puts it, they were to "fear God." That obedience, though, was not to be based on any effort to earn favor or anything else from the Lord. Rather, it was based on an already-established covenant relationship. *Because* God became Israel's Father at Sinai, Israel should trust that he has their best interests in mind. In the same way that I "feared" my own dad as a young child because I knew his instructions were for my good, God's people are to "fear" him because he is their Father and *acts* as a Father toward them. This goodness is exactly

---

40. Sandra Richter, *The Epic of Eden: A Christian Entry into the Old Testament* (Downers Grove, IL: IVP Academic, 2008), 73–75.

what Jesus was referring to when he compared God to human fathers:

> "What father among you, if his son asks for a fish, will give him a snake instead of a fish? Or if he asks for an egg, will give him a scorpion? If you then, who are evil, know how to give good gifts to your children, how much more will the heavenly Father give the Holy Spirit to those who ask him?"
>
> (Luke 11:11–13 CSB)

Okay, So What's the Point?

The point is that when Qohelet says that the "whole of humanity" is to "fear God and keep his commandments," he's saying that living in obedience to God as our Father is what it means to be human. The entire book drives toward this one point:

> *Despite the Abel-ness of the world, despite its unsteadiness and unpredictability, we can and should trust our Father to hold us fast.*

In all of life's ups and downs—in all of its terrible wonder and unimaginable pain and mystery—we can rest secure knowing that God loves us, that he's our Father. And further, this idea of living in obedient relationship gives us insight into the Qohelet's other advice for navigating a world turned upside down:

Enjoy God's gifts!

ENJOY GOD'S GIFTS

The Westminster Shorter Catechism says that humanity's "chief end is to glorify God and enjoy him forever." Before Westminster, the author of Ecclesiastes told us that God gave us gifts to enjoy—gifts, as we saw in chapter 1, that he gave Adam and Eve in the garden of Eden. This enjoyment of God's gifts is the second of the two-pronged response to this broken world that Ecclesiastes offers us.

We spent a little time in chapter 1 looking at the carpe diem passages: at the seven places in the book of Ecclesiastes where Qohelet tells us that we should enjoy some aspect of life, whether it's food, drink, a spouse, or work (2:24–26; 3:10–15, 16–22; 5:18–20; 8:10–15; 9:7–10; 11:8–10).

We also saw in chapter 1 that Qohelet didn't just choose these features of life at random. No, these are the very things Adam and Eve enjoyed when they were placed in the garden, when they had close fellowship with each other and with God, before that fateful day with the serpent.

This enjoyment of God's gifts is, in essence, a return to Eden. Thus, as we navigate this world marked by *hebel*, we can and indeed should embrace God's gifts to us as he allows.

There are two considerations to keep in mind as we think through Qohelet's admonition to enjoy God's gifts, both of which tether us to the "whole of humanity." First, these gifts are temporary and governed by God's sovereignty. Second, in this fallen world, these gifts are easily exploited by the sinful nature we inherited from our first parents.

Temporality and God's Sovereignty

Each of the gifts that Ecclesiastes mentions—food, work, wine, and a spouse—are brief and temporary. They do not last forever, and therefore they must be enjoyed *in the moment* that God allows their enjoyment. Once that slice of Chicago-style pizza is gone, it's gone. Once the workday is over, it's over. Once our conversation ends with our spouse, it ends. And once the bottle of wine is empty, it's empty. The temporal nature of these gifts therefore gives urgency to their enjoyment.

Furthermore, these gifts offer glimpses of our past life in the garden and our future life in the new heavens and new earth. In savoring taste and marital pleasure and a hard day of work, we simultaneously look back on life before sin and look forward to life after it.

These small pleasures are our day-to-day resistance of sin and darkness—and we can enjoy them at any moment and in any circumstance God allows. They offer hope as we anticipate the great wedding supper of the Lamb and the restoration of all things in God's kingdom. Since food, work, wine, and a spouse are only fleeting glimpses of the life to come, we must train our hearts to embrace the good God gives and resist discontentedness.

The second way these gifts connect us to God is that he exercises sovereignty over them. His sovereignty is assumed in how Ecclesiastes frames eating, drinking, working, and companionship: they are *gifts* from God, and therefore he controls who receives the gifts. Further, he also controls whether or not a person can actually take joy in his gifts. Qohelet is explicit regarding this relationship between God's giving of the gift itself and his allowing the enjoyment of it:

> Everyone to whom God has given riches and wealth, *he has also allowed him to enjoy them*, take his reward, and rejoice in his labor. This is a gift of God.
> (Eccl 5:19 CSB; emphasis added)

Just a few verses later, Qohelet frames God's sovereignty over enjoyment in the opposite way—sometimes he withholds the ability to enjoy the gift (which in 5:16 the author calls a "sickening tragedy"):

> God gives a person riches, wealth, and honor so that he lacks nothing of all he desires for himself, but God does not allow him to enjoy them.
> (Eccl 6:2 CSB)

As we enjoy life's fleeting pleasures, that very enjoyment points us back to the primary issue for Ecclesiastes: Living in right relationship with God or fearing him. Even the most quotidian of life's experiences—eating, drinking, working, and marriage—remind us that God is sovereign over all of life and also that he is *good*.

Guardrails Needed

God gave Adam and Eve a simple charge in Eden: Work and watch over this garden, enjoy each other ("be fruitful, multiply, fill the earth," Gen 1:28 CSB), and eat from all these plants and trees, but don't eat from this one tree. God's command was the guardrail—the protective element that would keep them from crashing over the edge into the depths of death. Of course, we know they transgressed, and now here we are trying to figure out how Ecclesiastes can help us navigate the treacherous waters we're still swimming in.

The fear of God *should* have kept Adam and Eve from eating from the tree of the knowledge of good and evil. In the same way, the fear of God provides guardrails as we enjoy his gifts today. There is an extreme on each side of these four gifts that we will tend toward if we do not fear God, and each of those extremes will rob us of the joy the gifts should bring.

God gives us food to enjoy, yet I have often found myself using it as a coping mechanism, a way to make me feel better when I'm sad. "Everything may be falling apart," I say, "but at least I can eat this entire pizza and feel a bit better about myself." My wife, on the other hand, struggles with the opposite extreme. "Everything may be falling apart," she says, "but at least I can steel myself against hunger."

Psalm 104 tells us that God gave "wine that makes human hearts glad" (v. 15 CSB). Unfortunately for me, however, I spent far too many years using alcohol to avoid *any* feelings, let alone being glad. On the other extreme, those who eschew alcohol in any and all circumstances miss out entirely on this gift of God. Of course, abstinence is much better than drunkenness, and the overuse of alcohol can lead to sexual violence, untimely death, and disease. Therefore, moderation in all things is key, and it's up to us to understand what's best for ourselves and those around us.

God also gives us work to provide for our families, as a creative outlet, and as a way to contribute to society and to love our neighbors. Yet the slothful person on the one extreme and the workaholic on the other both misuse the gift of work. We often don't think of work as a gift, but anyone in a long season of unwanted unemployment will tell you what a gift work is to us humans, and not only for the money that comes with it.

Finally, companionship, or a spouse, is the height of these good gifts from God. Some, however, choose to turn away from marriage, while others (like my own father) abuse it through adultery or other hurtful practices. For those who choose to remain celibate, there are good and right reasons for doing so, including clear biblical models on this issue. Nevertheless, the biblical message on the main is that marriage is a gift from God that should be enjoyed if God provides it.

In sum, Ecclesiastes teaches us how we can endure the Abel-ness of life, of reaching back to Eden and forward to eternal life, and of enduring sorrow and pain:

As fully as God allows, embrace the gifts he has given us of food, wine, work, and companionship.

These gifts go hand in hand with the Qohelet's summary: "Fear God and keep his commands." Instead of using his gifts as just another means of turning away from him, the fear of God shows us *how* to enjoy them.

THE END OF THE MATTER

Many years ago, I started out studying the book of Ecclesiastes because I thought I had found a fellow skeptic: someone like me who struggled to believe that the God of the Bible loved me and wanted to know me. I had read the book's pronouncement on life—"Everything is meaningless"—and I took comfort in the author's pessimism and nihilism. I'd been taught that Christians have to be happy, so you can imagine my relief at finding someone right there in the Bible who, like me, wasn't all that happy.

So, during my second or third year of seminary, I asked a professor to do an independent study with me on Ecclesiastes—and then I learned just how wrong I was. Qohelet was no nihilistic skeptic who declared everything meaningless; he wasn't even saying that everything is "meaningless without God." No, he was an orthodox wise man grappling with life in an upside-down world (as we saw chapters 1 and 2), trying his best to chart a path forward in the midst of significant anguish and sorrow (which we saw in chapter 3). That was exactly what I needed. I needed to see the fear of God as what it means to be a human being, and I needed to see enjoyment of God's gifts as glimpses of both Eden and the new heavens and the new earth.

Ecclesiastes hasn't taken away the devastation of losing my dad three times, and the death of my Mimi still stings. But this short book models an honest and faithful struggle with reconciling what God said in his word with what I—and maybe you too—experience in this life. Like I said before, if Ecclesiastes did *only* that, I would still be grateful for the fellow struggler I found. Graciously, however, Qohelet doesn't leave us with merely identifying and expressing the problem. Instead, he offers hope and comfort along the way:

Live in right relationship with God and enjoy the pleasures he gives us.

But on this side of the cross—and this is key for Christians reading Ecclesiastes—we can look back at this book and see more clearly what the author longed for. We know the harsh reality of living in the upside-down Abel-ness of this world, but we can also enjoy the temporal gifts God gives to us and more fully understand what it means to fear God—to trust him as our Father—because we know that *God became man*.

By his life, this God-man, Jesus Christ, showed that this world is indeed turned upside down, and like Abel (Gen. 4:10), Jesus' blood cries out. Unlike Abel, however, Jesus' blood doesn't cry out for justice. His blood cries out *as* justice, justice that reconciles sinners to God, that makes brothers out of enemies, that secures our place in God's great family.

So, friends, cling to the hope we have as God's adopted children who long for the day when Christ returns and finally sets this world aright!